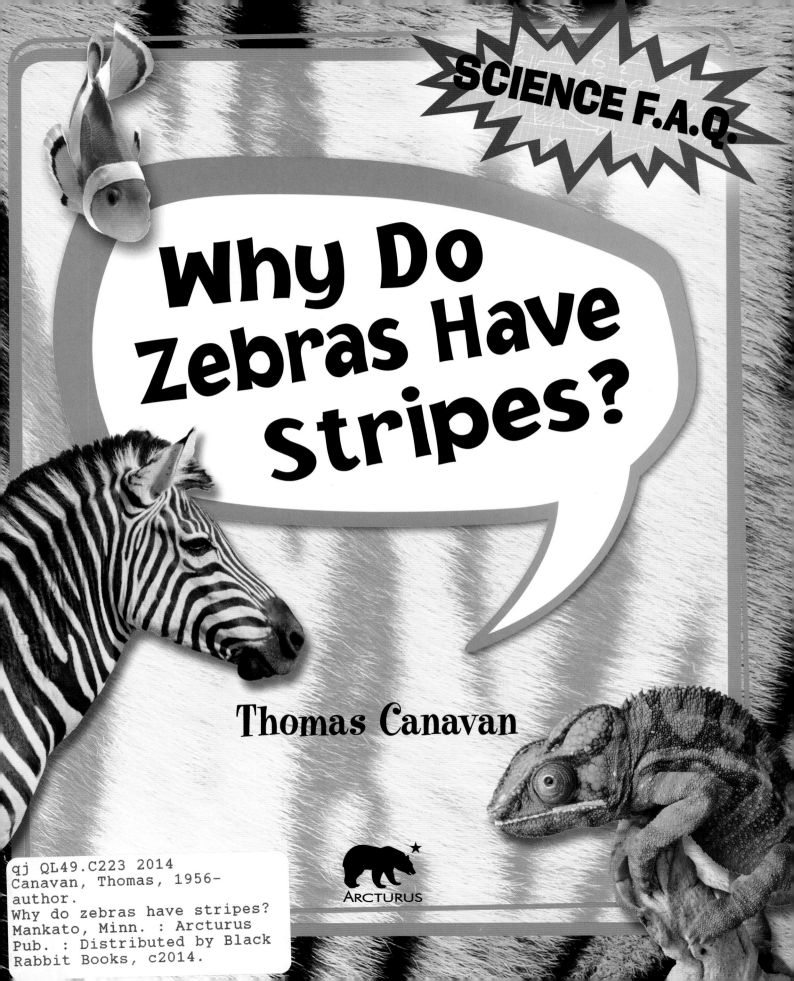

Why Do Zebras Have Stripes?

Thomas Canavan

ARCTURUS

This edition first published in 2014 by Arcturus Publishing

Distributed by Black Rabbit Books
P.O. Box 3263
Mankato
Minnesota MN 56002

Copyright © 2014 Arcturus Publishing Limited

Printed in China

Library of Congress Cataloging-in-Publication Data

Canavan, Thomas.
 Why do zebras have stripes? : questions and answers about animals / Thomas Canavan.
    p. cm. -- (Science FAQ)
 Summary: "Gives answers to common questions that kids have about animals"-- Provided by publisher.
 Includes index.
 ISBN 978-1-78212-397-2 (library binding)
 1. Animals--Miscellanea--Juvenile literature. 2. Children's questions and answers. I. Title.
 QL49.C223 2014
 590.2--dc23
                          2013005698

Editor: Joe Harris
Picture researcher: Joe Harris
Designer: Ian Winton

Picture credits:
All images supplied by Shutterstock, unless otherwise specified. The following images were supplied by
FLPA: page 8 top, page 9 top, page 16 top.

SL002664US
Supplier 03, Date 0513 Print Run 2366

Contents

Going for the record

These amazing animals are really taking things to the limit! They have the biggest teeth, the most legs ... or they're just huge. But would you dare to imagine what it would be like to meet some of these extreme creatures?

Why do centipedes have so many legs?

Centipedes need to be fast because they are hunters. The legs support their long bodies. They also help centipedes move quickly. A centipede's body is made up of lots of segments that are linked together. They're a little bit like trains. Each segment has a pair of legs.

What is or was the largest animal ever?

We've all seen pictures of the giant dinosaurs that lived millions of years ago. But the largest-ever animal is still around. The blue whale can grow to 108 feet (33 m) long and weigh 150,000 tons. But this ocean giant eats only tiny krill. Those are tiny shrimplike creatures the size of a jelly bean.

4

Which animal has the longest teeth?

Maybe you'd get this if the question asked for the longest tooth! That's because the longest single tooth belongs to the narwhal. The narwhal is a type of whale. One of its teeth can grow more than 10 feet (3 m) long. A narwhal uses its long tooth to impress other narwhals or even to battle rivals.

нарвал

10 K
10 KA

ПОЧТА СССР

1971

Why aren't land animals as **big** as they were in prehistoric times?

The largest dinosaurs lived when the Earth was warmer. It was easier for reptiles (including dinosaurs) to stay warm than it is now. That meant they could be bigger than modern reptiles. After the extinction of the dinosaurs, some mammals grew to a giant size. Human hunters probably caused the extinction of some of those large mammals.

What you see is what you get

Some animals are quick-change artists. Others look pretty weird to begin with. Take a look at some of these really wild animals. Can you explain to your friends why they look the way they do?

Why do zebras have stripes?

Scientists can't agree about the answer. Some say that the stripes help zebras blend into the background. Others claim that they make it easier for zebras to recognize each other. The latest idea is that stripes confuse bloodsucking flies. One thing they agree on is that zebras aren't white with black stripes. They're black with white stripes.

Why do elephants have big ears?

You might think that those ears help elephants hear really well. But their real job is to cool the elephant down. Warm blood flows through the many tiny blood vessels in the ears. Heat from the blood escapes through the skin into the outside air. That helps to keep the elephant from getting hot and bothered!

How do caterpillars become butterflies?

A caterpillar is a stage in the life cycle of a butterfly. It eats hungrily before attaching itself to a branch. Then it lets its outer layer drop away. Inside is a hard shell called a chrysalis. The cells in the chrysalis spend about two weeks changing into a new shape. The result is a butterfly, which breaks free of the chrysalis.

Can some animals really change color?

Some animals, such as chameleons, can change color quickly to hide from attackers or to send messages to each other. Other animals change color with the season. Hares, foxes, and other animals in the Arctic region have a white coat in the winter. That helps them blend into the snowy background.

7

All at sea?

How many times have you heard a story and thought it seemed fishy? Well, all of these stories are fishy ... but they're also true!

Do flying fish really fly?

These amazing fish don't really fly like birds. Instead, they're like hang gliders. They glide to escape from attackers. A flying fish builds up speed by wiggling its tail. It then launches from the water and spreads two long fins. These fins are like wings. They allow the fish to glide up to 1,300 feet (400 m) through the air.

Why do sharks have to swim all the time?

Most fish use a swim bladder to float. It's like a balloon. They fill the bladder with gas to float or empty it to sink. Sharks have no swim bladders. They use their fins like a plane's wings to go up or down. That means that they have to keep moving to keep floating!

Can you die if you touch an electric eel?

Electric eels store electricity in thousands of cells that are like batteries. They let off an electric charge to kill their prey or as self-defense. One of these bursts could hurt or even kill a human. Luckily, electric eels don't hunt humans. They usually hide when people are near.

Do fish sleep?

Yes they do, even if it's not like our own sleep. They have no eyelids, so they can't close their eyes. But fish do slow down to rest. Some fish just drift while they rest. Others snuggle into spaces between rocks or underwater plants. Sharks need to swim all the time, so they swim slowly as they rest.

Come to your senses

"I know that forest like the back of my paw." Can you imagine a bear or a dog saying that? You'd find out some pretty strange stuff if animals really could tell you how they find their way around.

Are bats really blind?

Some people think they're blind because they zigzag so much as they fly. But that's not because they can't see straight! It's because they are chasing insects. Bats also use other senses to hunt, including their fantastic sense of hearing.

Which animals have the best eyesight?

The animals with the sharpest eyesight are birds of prey that hunt during the day. Eagles, hawks, and falcons all rely on good eyesight. They need to spot prey as they fly high above the ground. An eagle can spot a hare up to 0.6 miles (1 km) away.

How can whales hear each other across an ocean?

Sound travels faster and longer in water than it does through the air. And low sounds, like whale calls, travel the farthest. The call of a blue whale is extremely low. It can travel thousands of miles— sometimes even across a whole ocean.

Why do some animals have more than two eyes?

Most large animals have two eyes. Simpler animals such as insects and jellyfish often have many more eyes. These allow them to see in many directions. Jumping spiders have eight eyes, four at the front and four at the back of the head, giving them good all-around vision.

11

Jurassic park life

The dial on this time machine must be broken. We can't have traveled back 100 million years, can we? Wait—what was that crunching sound, like crashing branches? It seemed to come from above us!
A-a-a dinosaur!

Do we know what color dinosaurs were?

For many years, scientists thought that dinosaurs were all gray, brown, or green. But recent discoveries show that some dinosaurs had feathers. Others probably had stripes. Feathers and stripes usually mean one thing—colors to attract or scare off other animals. But no one knows what those colors might have been.

How fast could the quickest dinosaurs run?

The group of dinosaurs called ornithomimids had long legs and could run at up to 50 miles per hour (80 km/h). The name ornithomimid means "bird mimic." They are called that because they looked like modern ostriches. Like these ancient relatives, ostriches use their long, powerful legs to run at high speed.

How **big** were the **largest** dinosaur eggs?

Dinosaurs were reptiles, and reptiles lay eggs. Chinese scientists uncovered the largest known dinosaur eggs in 2002. The eggs were 17 inches (43 cm) long and 5.7 inches (14.5 cm) wide. They belonged to a dinosaur called Macroelongatoolithus xixiaensis. This dinosaur lived about 100 million years ago.

Are birds related to dinosaurs?

Yes, they are. Scientists keep finding clues that make the link more obvious. In 2007, experts took some protein (a type of chemical found in living things) from a Tyrannosaurus rex. They compared it with protein from many modern animals. And the closest match was with a chicken!

Creepy-crawlies

It's amazing but true: four out of every five animals is an insect. And that's not even including spiders! Spiders don't get to be part of the insect club because they have eight legs, while insects only have six.

Do spiders ever get caught in their own webs?

Only if they're really unlucky. Not every strand of a web is sticky. Moths and other insects don't know which are and which aren't. That's why they get stuck when they fly into the web. But the spider remembers. It stays on the nonsticky strands as it walks across the web.

Why are moths attracted to light?

Moths use the Moon to help guide them at night. Bright lights—such as electric lights or candles—look a lot like the Moon, and this confuses them. As they fly along, they seem to be moving past the Moon, which shouldn't be possible! They keep changing direction to try to fly straight. But instead they fly closer and closer to the light.

Why don't flies fall off of ceilings?

Flies stick to ceilings because their feet produce a glue. The hard part is actually getting their feet off the ceiling! It's like when we try to walk across a muddy meadow. Flies usually keep two of their six legs off of the ceiling. They then have to peel each foot off—like peeling off a bandage—as they walk across.

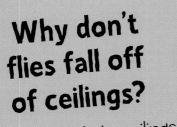

How long do adult insects live?

Insects go through several life stages—just think of caterpillars and butterflies. Some insects only live for a few days as adults. Adult mayflies have such a short life that they do not even have mouthparts for eating! But you can also find very old insects. A termite queen might live for more than 30 years.

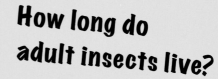

Yackety-yak

We humans can communicate in so many ways—text messages, emails, tweets, even old-fashioned talking! Have you ever wondered how animals pass on information to each other?

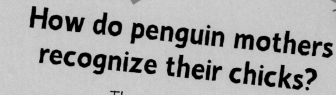

Do bees really talk to each other by dancing?

Honeybees live together in large hives. Some act like scouts and look for the best flowers to feed on. They return to the hive and do a "waggle dance." The direction of the dance tells others where to find the food.

How do penguin mothers recognize their chicks?

Thousands of penguins live in colonies near Antarctica. Mothers leave their nests to bring back food from the sea. But how do they recognize their own chicks among all the others when they return? They smell them! Penguins can tell the smell of their chicks (or their mates) even among those huge crowds.

Why do wolves **howl**?

Howling is usually a group effort, even if it starts with one wolf. Wolves live and hunt in packs. Howling is a way of getting the pack excited about going on a hunt—or it could celebrate a successful hunt. It might even be a way of telling other packs to stay away.

Can humans talk to dolphins?

Dolphins "talk" to each other with sounds such as clicks and whistles. Most of these sounds are either too high or too low for humans to hear. But Japanese scientists have produced a machine that might let us talk to dolphins. It can make—and hear—those high-pitched and low-pitched sounds. It might finally let humans talk to dolphins.

17

Baby creatures

There's a huge difference in the way animals are born. Some creatures, such as ocean sunfish, lay millions of eggs at a time. Others, such as elephants, give birth to one baby.

Why do kangaroos have pouches?

Kangaroos, like humans, are mammals. They give birth to live young. However, newborn kangaroos are tiny. They are less developed than most newborn mammals. After they are born, they spend another six to eight months in the mother's pouch. Then they are old enough to spend life outside it. Animals with pouches are called marsupials.

Why don't we ever see baby pigeons?

The simplest answer is that their parents spoil them. First of all, most city pigeon nests are hidden on top of buildings or bridges. But more importantly, baby pigeons stay in the nests for a long time. Their parents keep bringing them food. By the time they leave, they look almost like adults.

Can dogs be bred back into wolves?

Yes, they can. Dogs are the descendants of wolves. They sometimes look very different, but they can still have offspring together. The puppy of a wolf and a dog is called a wolfdog. A wolfdog mating with a wolf would produce puppies that were three-quarters wolf.

Do any mammals lay eggs?

Most mammals give birth to live young. But platypuses and four species of anteater—all living in or near Australia—lay eggs. They're still called mammals, though. That's because they have hair and also because the mothers produce milk to feed their young.

19

What's for dinner?

At school, we learn about having a balanced diet and eating the right things. Most animals, though, must find the right balance between finding food ... and not being eaten themselves!

How do snakes breathe while they swallow their prey?

Snakes can swallow prey that's very wide. They would choke if this food blocked air from getting into their windpipe. But they can stretch the windpipe along the bottom of their mouth. The end of it comes out in front of the food. So the snake can breathe even while it takes its time swallowing.

Can piranhas really strip the flesh off a cow in minutes?

Piranhas are small South American fish with sharp teeth. And yes, a swarm of them really could devour a large animal in minutes. But they usually stick to eating worms, insects, and small fish. And they don't usually swarm to attack. They gang up to defend themselves against attackers.

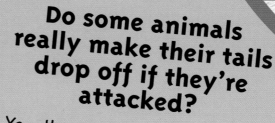

Do some animals really make their tails drop off if they're attacked?

Yes, they do! Some lizards have joins on their tails. They can make their tail drop off if they are in danger from a predator. The tail wiggles around for a few seconds. That's often long enough to fool an attacker into letting them escape. The lizards can grow another tail, but the new tail can't drop off.

Is chocolate poisonous to dogs?

Yes, and they can die from eating too much of it. Chocolate contains theobromine. That chemical is poisonous to many animals— even humans. But we can break it down and make it harmless. Dogs can't, so the poison builds up inside them. Dark chocolate has lots of theobromine. About 2.5 ounces (70 g) could kill a small dog.

Up and away

Have you ever looked up at birds and thought, "I'd love to be able to fly?" Just imagine what it must really be like to take to the air and soar around for hours.

Can birds sleep in midair?

Swifts can spend more than a year in the air. That's from the moment they leave the nest until they return to breed. They have small midair naps. Some people believe that albatrosses must also sleep in midair. These huge seabirds only come to shore to breed. They would be attacked if they slept on the water.

How can birds sit on power lines without being killed?

The birds survive because the electricity in the power lines has no reason to pass through them. A copper wire is easier to pass through than a bird, so the electricity stays in the wire. However, the birds could die if they were touching the wire at the same time as touching something else.

22

What's the largest flock of birds?

The largest recorded flock of birds was in southern Canada in 1866. A flock of passenger pigeons about 1 mile (1.6 km) wide passed overhead. It took 14 hours for the flock to pass by. It was judged to be 300 miles (500 km) long. And the flock contained 3.5 billion birds. Sadly, passenger pigeons became extinct in 1914.

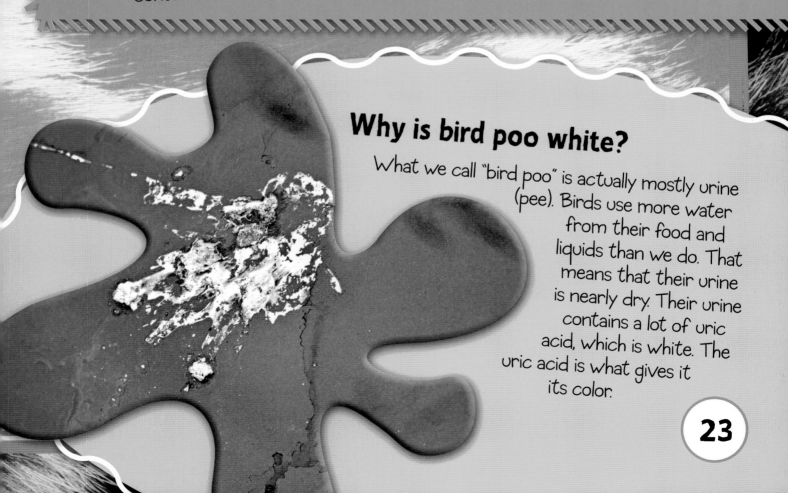

Why is bird poo white?

What we call "bird poo" is actually mostly urine (pee). Birds use more water from their food and liquids than we do. That means that their urine is nearly dry. Their urine contains a lot of uric acid, which is white. The uric acid is what gives it its color.

Fact or fiction?

We've heard so many crazy stories about animals that it's hard to tell which are true and which are legends. Now it's time for you to become a detective and discover the truth.

Do vampire bats really drink blood?

These natives of North and South America do drink blood, but they're not really dangerous. First of all, they're afraid of humans. Second, they don't drink much blood from the cows and horses they land on. They make a shallow bite with their sharp teeth. Then they take about a thimbleful of blood. It's more like a mosquito bite than Dracula.

Did unicorns ever exist?

The unicorn was supposed to be a white horse with a long straight horn jutting out from its head. Ancient travelers probably saw long-horned antelopes from the side and thought they were unicorns. In late 2012, the mysterious leaders of North Korea said that they had found unicorn skeletons. But scientists still don't believe that the story is true.

24

Do elephants really go to an "elephants' graveyard" when they're dying?

Legends tell of a place where old elephants go to die. Anyone discovering it would find a huge pile of elephant bones, including tusks that could be sold as ivory. In reality, there's no such place. But there's a little truth behind the legend. Strong African winds sometimes blow elephant bones into piles.

Do cats really have nine lives?

Cats have only one life, like all living creatures. But this is another legend that is based on a little truth. Cats are able to walk away from falls that would hurt or kill other animals. They have incredible balance and can sometimes fall from skyscrapers without getting hurt. It's not surprising that people think that they have nine lives.

25

Just like us?

Everyone gives their teddy bear or stuffed bunny a name. And we read stories about toads driving cars or bears writing poetry. But how much like people are animals in real life?

Do hibernating animals ever oversleep?

No, they don't! Loud noises or bright lights don't wake them up. They're roused by chemical signals. A part of the brain called the hypothalamus notices falling temperatures or darkening days in the fall. It then "sets the alarm" for an exact number of days. The body produces the wake-up chemical after that many days.

Do seals and whales get seasick?

People and animals get seasick because their brains get confused. Their eyes tell them that they're sitting still. But sensors inside their ears can tell that they're moving up and down on the sea. Seals and whales can see—and sense—that they're moving. With no confusion, they don't get seasick.

Do animals have belly buttons?

Yes, but only mammals. That's the group of animals that includes us. Nearly all mammals develop inside their mothers before they're born. During that time, they get food through a tube that goes into their stomach. Once mammals are born, they don't need that tube anymore. It drops off. All that's left is a little scar—the belly button.

Do lions purr like pet cats?

Scientists divide the cat family into those that purr and those that roar. Your pet cat has small bones at the back of its tongue. They lead to the skull. These bones make the purring sound when the cat vibrates its throat. Lions and other "roarers" lack those little vibrating bones. But they can open their throats wider to make their loud roars.

It's roundup time

By now you should be able to convince your friends that you're an expert on animal life. If they don't believe you, prove it by rattling off some of these weird and wonderful animal facts.

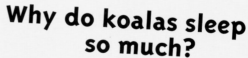

What do camels store in their humps?

Those lumps are stores of fatty tissue. They're like batteries to give the camel energy and water when it can't eat or drink. Storing fat in lumps is better for a desert animal than having fat covering the whole body. That would make the animal too hot.

Why do koalas sleep so much?

Koalas don't have a very good diet. They eat only the leaves of eucalyptus trees. And those leaves don't give the koalas much energy. So the koala spends a lot of time asleep. Luckily, it has no predators that could attack it ... or disturb its sleep.

How do bats find their way around in the dark?

Bats use a sense called "echolocation" to move around and to find insect food. They make lots of squeaks. Then their sensitive ears pick up the echoes of the squeaks and can tell exactly where it came from. They use the echoes to build up a picture of the world around them.

Are animals ticklish?

Scientists have known for a long time that some animals are definitely ticklish. Our closest relatives—gorillas and monkeys—squirm and laugh like humans. Now it seems that other animals are ticklish, too. A scientist asked a student to tickle a rat as a joke. They were both surprised when the rat wriggled its legs and squeaked—just like laughing.

29

Glossary

balance this word is used in two different ways: 1) a situation in which different things are in equal or the right amounts, and 2) being able to stay upright

blood vessel one of the many tubes carrying blood through a body

charge a transfer of electrical force

colonies large groups of animals living close together

communicate to share or exchange information

descendants Children, grandchildren, great-grandchildren, and so on

diet the type and amount of food someone or something eats

extinction when there are no longer any living members of a species of animal, plant, or some other once-living thing

hibernating sleeping through the winter

impress to make others think better of you

ivory a hard, yellowish-white substance that makes up an elephant's tusk

life cycle the pattern of birth, growing, and death of an animal or plant

mammal an animal that gives birth to live young, which get milk from their mother

marsupial a type of mammal that gives birth to tiny young, which stay in a pouch on the mother

mimic an animal that can match the look or sound of something else

pitch the measure of how high or low a sound is

predator an animal that feeds on other animals

prehistoric in the time before people began to keep written records

prey an animal that is hunted by another animal

protein a special chemical that animals need to live

reptile an egg-laying animal that is covered in hard scales

segment one of the parts of something

skeleton a set of connected bones that supports an animal

squirm to twist around

tissue tiny connected parts of the body that do a certain job

waggle to move with short, quick motions

windpipe a tube carrying air from the mouth or nose to the lungs

Further Reading

100 Deadliest Things on the Planet by Anna Claybourne (Scholastic Paperbacks, 2012)

Dogs and Cats by Steve Jenkins (Sandpiper, 2012)

National Geographic Animal Encyclopedia: 2,500 Animals with Photos, Maps, and More! by Lucy Spelman (National Geographic Children's Books, 2012)

Ocean (Lifecycles) by Sean Callery (Kingfisher, 2011)

Web Sites

Animal Information
www.seaworld.org/animal-info/index.htm
The Animal section of the SeaWorld web site is aimed at young people and goes far beyond the world of maritime creatures. Thorough information on all kinds of animal-related subjects is backed up with interactive features—especially the constantly updated set of animal sound files.

Kids' Planet
www.kidsplanet.org/
Organized by the Defenders of Wildlife, this colorful interactive site is packed with information about animals—habitats, diversity, conservation, and much more. Plus there's a cool howling wolf to greet you as you enter the site.

National Geographic: Animals
http://animals.nationalgeographic.com/animals/?source=NavAniHome
The National Geographic's Animal section subdivides into a number of areas, from facts, photos, and videos, to animal conservation and weird and wonderful news stories. An excellent site with high-quality learning materials.

Smithsonian National Zoo
http://nationalzoo.si.edu/Animals/AnimalIndex/
This web site has a wealth of fact sheets and photo galleries for the Smithsonian National Zoo's 2,000 individual animals from nearly 400 different species. It features amazing live web cams of many of the animals and links to other educational sites.

Index